Run

Written & Illustrated By:
Lorraine K. Toth
Cover Art: Lorraine K. Toth

DEDICATION

Dedicated to my babies - my hearts and soul: Shawnee and Johnny. You gave my life purpose. You show me unconditional love.

To the women who doubt themselves and feel helpless - you've got this! You are not alone and it does get better. Take this time to break open to a new and better YOU!

*In life you will make wrong decisions and wrong turns. The important thing is that you get back on the path that feels good to **YOU**.*

Lorraine K. Toth

Chapter One

I lean back against a huge tree and stretch, trying to ease my anxiety as much as I hoped to loosen my muscles in the cool morning air. "I should pee," I think, not knowing how long it would be before I would have another opportunity to go once the race started.

On my way out of the ladies' room, I eat the apple I brought with me for a quick boost of extra energy, taking in the sights around me. People are standing in groups with their running partners, talking excitedly, anxious to get the race started – if I didn't know what we were here for, I might think we're standing around at some kind of social event, like a concert or party. I feel a smile slowly find my mouth – I'm really here! I'm doing this with all of these people! Except, I'm not really here with them. I'm alone. I'm just like an outside observer taking in this whole scene.

I shake my head. "Focus!" I have a goal and I'm going to crush it. I'm going to prove I can do this. I'm going to listen to my body and use the power of my mind to fuel myself straight through to the finish line!

***

What is Your Body Telling You?

Your body gives you clues. If you are like I was though, you ignore these warning signs or red flags and carry on with your daily life. You try to trick yourself and think it'll get better or maybe you cover up that migraine with some Tylenol. You get a massage to temporarily ease the tension in your shoulders. You take a vacation to escape the stress, temporarily. Eventually though, your body is taken over and stricken with pain or disease and you can no longer ignore these fires within.

That is what happened to me in 2012.

My body literally felt like it was on fire. I sat upright and writhed in bed in pain. I was unable to leave the room and was barely able to make it to the bathroom without collapsing in pain. I had these strange red marks on my right hip that looked like I burnt myself or wore clothing that was too tight. I wanted to block the pain with Tylenol or Advil or anything, but nothing could mask the pain of this horrible attack on my body. I had no choice but to lie in bed screaming out for outside help, not yet realizing the only help I needed was within.

I went to my family doctor who diagnosed me with Shingles. I was only 36 years old - how could I have shingles? It was a disease that only old people got, or so I thought. The doctor offered no insight as to why I had shingles and said that there were no drugs to cure this attack on my body and that I just had to wait it out. Western medicine at its best!

Well, I was not happy with this lack of explanation, however! Some call me stubborn, but I knew that everything has a cause and that there is always a holistic way of treating disease. I went to the ever-trusted Google and researched shingles looking for an answer. To me, this situation was like an analogy. "If your house is on fire, do you just disconnect the smoke alarm and wait it out, or do you listen to the alarm and do something to put out the fire?"

Hell yes, you put out the fire! So I went on a mission to figure out how to put out the fire in my body and cure the shingles.

Through my research, I found out that Eastern medicine has been using Acupuncture for years to treat shingles! They believe that shingles is caused due to an imbalance in the body's yin and yang.

I reflected inward. I thought of how my life was in constant turmoil because of my unhappy marriage. I recognized that all of the pain and hurt I was experiencing consistently, all of the biting of my tongue and avoiding when I really wanted to speak my mind, was causing me to bury so much negativity in me that my body was unbalanced. Of course! It made complete sense to me that by harboring all of this blackness in my life rather than dealing with it, my body was sending out a clear S.O.S. and announced "What the fuck? You need help bitch!" And it was coming out in the form of shingles.

The fire from within my body equated the fire I had been covering up inside. Each time I failed to speak my mind to my husband, each time I did something against my choice, each time I told myself, "maybe he will change", and each time I was saddened by the lack of affection within our marriage, I sent the wrong message to my body. I was telling my body through my actions that *I* didn't matter.

But you can only fool yourself for so long before the genius system that guides us stands up and raises that red flag!

I made an appointment for Acupuncture with a doctor who had practiced in China. With only a couple of visits, my shingles was "cured" and it has not returned. With only two visits, she got my body's yin and yang back in balance, and my red streaks and pain faded. And just remember - I was told by my family doctor that there was NO treatment for shingles. Had I listened to modern medicine I would have been writhing in pain and possibly still having these horrendous red streaks along my hips and abdomen!

This experience has lead me to believe that Western medicine focuses on covering up the symptom rather than curing the cause of the problem. Instead of accepting your doctor's prescription for a pain killer or an antibiotic, stop for a moment and ask yourself: "Why do I have these symptoms?" Look at your lifestyle. What is your personal life like? What is your stress level? What is your diet like?

If Western Medicine does not have a solution for you, look into holistic or Eastern medicine. Doctors and pharmaceutical companies are in it to make money. Or sometimes, they simply do not have the training or all of the facts to properly guide you.

Don't be afraid to think outside of the box, to search for answers to YOUR problem - you are an individual so if they try to "blanket" treat your symptoms and provide you with a prescription or solution simply because it is what they do for all of their patients - think twice. The answers are out there; you may just have to do some digging. You are the advocate for your body, not them.

***

The Relationships You Keep

STOP! Listen to the signs your body is giving you!

Your body will give you signs in all aspects of your life – not just your physical health.

Do you experience a nervous shake when your husband or wife is about to come home? Do you get anxious? Do you have tension headaches when he or she is in the room? Do you clench your jaw or grind your teeth? Do you feel your pulse quicken? Do you quickly clean up the house in order to avoid another argument? Do you hide your excitement or act less happy to match their mood? Do you give up what you really want to do in order to keep the peace?

I did all of the above. It got me nowhere, except sick, unhappy and older. I tried to fool myself into thinking I could change to save the marriage. I tried to become someone I was not.

I was outside running the summer before this marathon to train, and I heard the words from a rap song by Lauren Hill echo into my ears and resonate throughout my body: "I am not your expectations". I could completely relate to these words as I ran a little faster through the back roads of Lake Nancy in Upstate NY.

In couples' therapy, I would hear about how I was too artistic and too free of a spirit and how I was not responsible. I would hear how I needed to be more black and white. My free form way of thinking did not plan properly for the future. Through desperation and hope of keeping my family together, I tried to dim the light that shined within me and stray from my artistic train of thought. I dulled the creative paintings that would float into my head, the pages of a book I wanted to write, the T-shirt designs I dreamed up and the businesses I wanted to start and instead – I focused on a simple 9 to 5 train of thought that I knew would make my husband happier.

This would put a Band-Aid on us for a week or so where we could exist less in conflict. However, it would cause me so much angst for trying to live by another's set of rules.

I began to feel dead inside. I noticed my jaw ached from biting my tongue so much when I wanted to say what I thought and instead said what he wanted to hear. I noticed I was tired and felt like I had the weight of the world on my shoulders. My massage therapist said my shoulder and neck area was so knotted up it would take weeks to undo the tension.

I binge ate, trying to fill the void in my relationship. If I did do a little painting, I hid it from him in fear of angering him that I had once again acted all "artistic".

I kept journals for our entire 9-year relationship. They are mostly filled with negativity and each entry basically started with: "He and I are fighting again"; or "we aren't talking, I did xyz to piss him off". I didn't know at the time, but focusing on all of the negatives in the relationship and by continuously saying "I don't want this anymore", I was sending out the wrong messages.

This is BULLSHIT, I finally realized. The more you hide who you are, the more you put out that fire within, and you slowly die. This is not living. I realize now that I had to try to save the marriage by acting out the part of "HIS perfect wife". I had to know deep down inside that I did try everything, and it still would not work. The minute I gave myself permission to be who I truly was, however, it all began to change.

Chapter Two

I line up at the starting line with the other 2,458 racers in the marathon. I'm near the front of the pack, because they've lined us up according to our starting paces.

As I wait for the gun to go off to start the race I send out a wish to the universe that the three health practitioners and the running coach were all wrong when they told me my body wasn't ready. They all warned me that I would not be prepared for this and I would end up injured. My running coach, Paul Stevens, who gently guided me from making it through a 5k to where I was now kindly suggested "maybe next year". I knew I couldn't wait until next year though. I needed this marathon badge now. All of these experts said my asthma would keep me from finishing, or that my body would shut down or I would "hit the wall" which is a famous runner's term of having to quit a race. They all separately agreed I would be injured or suffer long term consequences from pushing myself to the extremes so soon.

I wasn't going to let them be right. I know the farthest I ran during my training sessions was a whopping 9 miles – and today I'm here expecting my body to do three times that distance. I was a poor student and did not even closely follow my coach's running plan of exact mileage tapering. I know it's actually insane for me to be here right now.

I visualize myself crossing the finish line over and over in my head, just like I had done for weeks during my meditation practice. I know my "mental training" will help compensate for my lack of actual running training. That, and my motivation and desire to prove myself... and run myself right to a new life. I'm going to accomplish this. I am going to finish all 26.2 miles of this marathon.

"All relationships are a mirror onto ourselves."

- Deepak Chopra

I recently pulled out a sheet of free form writing and thought processing from almost 3 years ago (pre-divorce). I was shocked to see how dark my mind really was. There was a lot of negative thoughts and statements on the paper. A lot of confusion and pain. It is so helpful to be able to go back and reflect on where you were to where you are now. If you are stuck in your head and thoughts are whirling around I encourage you to pull out a large sheet of blank paper and just write whatever pops into your head on the paper. Do not filter it.

Another helpful project is to write a letter to your younger self. Tell yourself what you have learned. Pretend you can go back in time and be the wiser version of the younger you. My letter to myself was quite illuminating. Things I had put on the back burner of my mind came to me like a spotlight on how much I really had learned. I realized how wise I had become through all of the wrong turns and mishaps. Things that went "not according to plan" were because I needed to learn for myself - about mistrust, self doubt, the search for perfection and so on.

Following is my letter to myself. I found it so therapeutic to be honest about all that I have endured. I read it the first time and had a tear come to my eye. To some reading it I am sure you will think it a miracle I am sane. I read it now and realize what a strong woman I am. I am confident I can help others as I have conquered more than the average person. My life is a fucking Lifetime movie!

Dear Beautiful:

As you stand there shaking and unsure of yourself, just know - this too shall pass. The doubt you have daily will be replaced with a confidence that only a woman who has lived through hell and risen above can radiate.

Throughout your adolescence while living at home you will hide yourself in your art. It will be the escape and source of peace when your daily home life is a place of dysfunction. The love you deserve from your father will never come until about twenty years later. You will fear him when he is near. Your pulse will quicken when he is in the room. Your body will develop a fight or flight response. At twelve years old you will find your voice and shout out in your defense that you will never be hit again or the cops will be called.

You will move out the exact day you get your high school diploma and instantly search for the white picket fence dream your childhood lacked. You will try to replace the love you lacked from your father figure with a boy you were engaged to in high school. You try to grow up too quickly from 18 to 20, all of this because you are unaware that you are trying to cover up the hole in your heart and the painful memories.

In your early twenties when you are a depressed, overweight new, young mom in an unfulfilling marriage you will begin to push the limits in search for happiness. You will move out with your new baby, divorce your husband of two years at the young age of twenty to go date the sixteen-year older man. The Greek god looking type who oozes sex and makes you feel alive will also make you doubt yourself constantly to the point of plastic surgery, working out three hours a day and counting every single calorie. The older man who cheats on you constantly, who you take a gun out of his hands, who knocks himself unconscious when you try to break up with him and have to call 911 for will show you what you do not want and deserve. This older man who you have arrested and a restraining order placed upon will teach you what it is like to stand up for yourself. The twenties teach you extremes and the ugliness in searching for perfection.

In your thirties, you will realize perfection is not an outward thing. It is your vision of yourself that matters. You can be the most flawless bikini model on the outside but a crumbled up ball of anxiety on the inside. Even when you will be competing in international figure competitions on a stage in a bikini for thousands to judge, when your body is "picture perfect" in your mid-twenties - you will feel sexier later in life. The woman with stretch marks from baring two amazing babies, cellulite, pale white skin, a few white hairs and wrinkles sprouting as you approach forty will feel way hotter. Knowing you have so much more to offer than what shows on the outside will make you feel like a supermodel, I promise you.

Your thirties will also teach you that you can only control yourself. You will get married again and once again strive for your white picket fence dream. You will admire this man who challenges you and is the intellectual relationship you desired. You will pretend to be someone you are not to keep the peace. You will try to fool yourself that you are happy but your body will show you signs that this is not so. Eventually after years of unhappiness you two will part and finally the growth that had been building for years will happen. You will finally break open. You will heal. You will also learn the power of forgiveness. This will allow the blackness that you harbored for years to leave your body. It was poison to you. You will feel lighter when you let it go. Gone will be the days when you pick yourself apart in the mirror and rely what others tell you. Gone will be the days when you doubt your intuition when someone you love lies to you. Gone will be the days when you need the reassurance of a man. All you need will come from within. The calm, centered focus will burn brightly and you will know you love yourself as you are. Finally, the day will come and you will need no one else's approval other than your own.

Until then, don't beat yourself up. Life is a journey, not a destination. Every mistake will point you towards the road you were meant to be on. Learn from each "re-direction" of your life. Cry your heart out when you are hurt and heartbroken. Don't hold it in like you are used to doing. Don't put on the fake happy face when inside you are crumbling. Don't pretend you can do it all on your own. Write in that journal you have kept since you were twelve. You will look back on those diaries someday and realize how strong you really were and are still. Learn about yourself. Set goals and conquer them. Give gratitude for what you are grateful for and more of what you desire will surely enter your life. You will become spiritual in your late thirties. You will take classes on this and learn to live more Zen and mindful. Keep up with the meditation. Quiet your mind. Don't become emotionally attached to thoughts as they enter your head. Instead, all them to enter and then go out. You got this!

Enjoy your journey,

Lorraine

***

Run towards a new you.

The runners around me start taking off some of their layers, tossing their long sleeve shirts to the ground at the side of the road. I knew this was a common marathon practice, so I came prepared. You need the extra layer early in the morning when the weather is still cool, but as soon as you start running your body will heat up quickly. I peel my hot pink, long sleeved t-shirt off and donated it to the cause as well. After all of the runners have moved away from the starting line, people will come along and gather up all of our donated shirts and bring them to homeless shelters.

The gun goes off. Together with thousands of runners, I begin my 26.2-mile journey. I feel great. I listen to my breath, a steady in and out rhythm. I hear the feet of runners behind me as they hit the ground. The scenery of Lake Champlain is peaceful and the morning sun is starting to warm me up. This is like a pleasure cruise – not a race! "I'm invincible!" I think. The runner's high is setting in, and for the first 13.1 miles I don't even turn on my music, I just focus on the sound of my breath.

***

I used to think that the 13.1 or 26.2 stickers I saw on the back of cars were for radio stations. Well, I am determined to earn those radio station stickers and then some! Despite countless doctors over the course of my life telling me I could not run because of my asthma, I am out here running – and not only can I do it, but it turns out – I'm pretty damn good at it!

It's amazing, really. It's not an easy thing to go from barely being able to walk up a hill without getting all out of breath, to training for a FULL marathon, let me tell you! Most of what you need to overcome a challenge is all in your head. You know the whole "mind over matter" thing? It is the absolute truth. Once you really believe you can do something, then your body will complete the task you assign.

Food: Are You Eating Poison or Fuel?

I grew up with horrible asthma. The last couple of years, before I changed my diet and starting on my running journey, I was in and out of urgent care, ER, asthma specialists, and my primary doctor. I was spending thousands of dollars on inhalers, nebulizers, prednisone and other anti-inflammatories. I would spend vacations lying in bed instead of actually out enjoying myself. I was walking around tired and hunched over because I could not get enough air in.

I am not sure what triggered me to look deeper, but I got tired of living like that. My doctors and modern medicine practices told me to take daily medicine to prevent my asthma attacks. Their theory was that by taking a medication 365 days a year I could prevent the approximately 14 days of actual suffering I experienced when I had an asthma attack. When I stopped to think about this, it really didn't make sense to me to take something all the time that I really only needed some of the time! I also didn't like the side effects of these drugs - especially the shakiness I got when I took the inhalers or nebulizers. The oral medications like Prednisone... well don't even get me started on their side effects, which included bloating!

I didn't like the answers the doctors were giving me. And, since I'm stubborn, I decided to look elsewhere for a cure or treatment that better relieved my symptoms. I knew there had to be other options, and if I searched long enough I would discover something that worked better for me. And I did. I found that I could relieve my asthma symptoms and help my body become more in balance through diet changes.

Do yourself a favor and Google "functional medicine" and "Dr. Hyman". So many of you will see your spine specialist or your cardiologist or your skin doctor or your asthma specialist for the things that trouble you. And all of these doctors and specialists will offer their own approach that basically come down to the same thing. Modern medicine tends to cover up your symptoms rather than treat the actual problem.

For me, inflammation was my body's way of trying to help me breathe. My doctor tried to cover up and suppress the inflammation.

Try looking at your physical ailments, or even other complications such as anxiety and depression, from a different perspective. Look for common causes - animals, mold, food allergies, etc. What triggers the symptom? If you can figure out what triggers the symptom you want to avoid, and then treat the cause of the symptom, you'll have better results than taking a medication to try and cover up the symptom or provide temporary relief from it.

For me, treating the cause of my symptoms required eliminating gluten from my diet, and staying away from allergens that cause inflammation and lack of breath. I had to take out the stuff that is bad for my body and put in what it needs, so my body could figure it out and start to improve itself.

I'm not a doctor or an expert on this matter, but I speak from my personal experience that it completely turned my life and physical health around. So if you've been trying the traditional medicine ways and not finding the relief you want, why not give functional medicine a try and see if it works for you, too?

Other common food allergies include soy, corn, dairy, and peanut butter. And not all allergies result in the need for an Epipen and a trip to the ER for anaphylaxis. You can be allergic to foods in other ways. For me, I learned peanut butter is a migraine trigger. I did the Dr. Hyman "Elimination Diet" and found out the source of my recurring migraines was from eating a couple spoonful's of peanut butter straight out of the jar!

If you crave something, is your body lacking something? Consider how you feel after you eat certain foods. Are there bumps on your arms? Does your face break out only in one area? These are all signs that you probably shouldn't be eating something. Your body is trying to show you that you aren't giving it what it needs to function healthfully.

Lorraine K. Toth

Chapter Three

I started running with my husband (at the time, he's now my ex-husband) as something we could do together and a goal we could share. While I no longer have the husband, I still have the goal! I remember my first time running with him, I needed frequent breaks and my pace was around a 15-minute mile. Sadly, I couldn't even make it one single mile without needing to take a break and walk to catch my breath. Fast forward two years later, and I am able to look back and reflect through my handy "Runkeeper" app on my iPhone, and see that I pretty much not only increased my pace to about half the time (I can do an 8 min 30 sec mile now) but I have also drastically increased my distance.

***

I used to think that 26.2 miles would be impossible and those marathon people were insane! As my feet continue to hit the pavement in a steady rhythm two hours into this marathon – I realize I am now one of them.

Now, a few hours into this marathon, my feet are absolutely killing me. When I can take the pain no more, I sit down on the side of the trail to readjust my socks and figure out what's causing the pain. There is blood starting to come through the sock on one of my toes from the constant friction of the sock against my sneaker. I've got painful blisters forming all over my feet. I assess the damage, put my socks back on, and lace back up. I can't let a little foot pain stop me from finishing this race.

There is so much time to think out here. I'm thankful for that, since my mind is what's keeping me going!

In the beginning I joined a running club and ran a few 5k races to get into the mental mindset and commit to becoming a runner. I ran my first race with my daughter, who was 17 at the time, and who is an avid cross country runner. Thankfully, she ran by my side each of the 3 races we did together rather than leaving me in the dust! She gave me tips like "don't cross your arms across your body, keep 90 degree angles"; "regulate your breathing"; "pick someone in front of you and catch up to them"; and "lean forward when going uphill".

When I crossed my very first finish line in the Friehoffer's Race for Women, I was so elated! My daughter and I even finished within the top 15% of the thousands of women who ran the 5k. That feeling of accomplishment is something I was able to bring with me into other aspects of my life.

This is the real story I want to share with you. It's not so much about the marathon itself, or how I accomplished a physical activity. It's how you can take a physical activity like running, and carry the things you learn throughout the process and your accomplishments over into other areas of your daily life.

In fact, it's more about what you learn throughout the process, and the mental strength you achieve than it is the physical goal of being able to complete a marathon or some other physical activity you set your sights on.

I'm hoping that by reading this book, I can show you that you CAN do what you desire. You CAN change the patterns and routines in your life to accomplish new things, overcome challenges, and reach your own goals. You CAN overcome health issues or the labels you have had since birth. Did someone tell you that you couldn't do something? That's a label. I had a label my whole life until this moment – I was told my asthma would prevent me from running. I decided to get rid of that label and change my thinking to overcome that physical limitation, and in the process, I learned I can get rid of negative thoughts and energy and reach other goals I never dreamed possible. YOU can get rid of negative or black energy, too, and live a life of fulfillment and reach goals you have never thought possible.

I can offer this perspective as I learned how to do all of this while simultaneously overcoming the dark, dark, sad and horribly painful days of early divorce. It is my hope that sharing my experience will shed some light onto your situation and help lift you up to accomplish your own goals.

If you are like me, you thumb through self-help books looking for a story or an author you can relate to. I want to give women and men going through life's challenges a new viewpoint that yes, you *can* make it up that hill. And that just over the top of that hill, even when it seems so far, far away - you can find **yourself** and learn who you are. You not only see the finish line - you see a new perspective and run towards a new life. You don't have to be that sobbing, penniless hot mess!!!! You don't have to accept life however it is for you right now, if it's not what you want it to be.

You can RUN THROUGH LIFE, even during times when you feel as though you cannot breathe.

Signs from Above

While on the phone in NYC with my attorney, she made it clear what my legal options were. I made the decision right there to go completely against that legal plan. She was doing exactly what I hired her to do. But there are times when we need to take in the advice of others, check in with how that feels to us and trust our intuition. I chose to do what my heart told me to do and haven't looked back. I got off the phone and told my friend, Tenicia, who was with me at the time that I couldn't do as they were counseling me. The abruptness of me making this life altering decision caused the universe to give me my first ever "heart shape" sign. It was my first time being lucky enough to have the reassurance that I was on the right path by something grander than I.

A heart shaped blood stain appeared on my underwear. My period wasn't due for another week but here I was with a perfectly shaped red heart in my thong. I showed my friend in disbelief and she spoke of women's tribes that "worship" these types of signs. It was as I had thought, a peaceful sign from above that everything would be ok.

I have since seen too many heart shapes to count over the years. They always appear when I am doubting a decision or feeling down. They have become my road map. I express such gratitude when one appears in my morning coffee mug, an eggshell, a water stain, a rock, a splatter of paint and so on. The most beautiful one I have ever seen however is the two perfectly shaped hearts that appeared in my snow covered driveway last winter.

Watch for these road maps in your own life. It may not be heart shapes for you. Maybe it's a numerical sequence you see often, etc. Just pay attention and be open. It is bigger than you so accept this guidance from above with grace.

Chapter Four

It's getting so hot now, the combination of running for hours and being out in the open in the pure sun with no shade. I slow down a bit as I see several people lying flat on their backs with EMTs surrounding them. Will that be me? I wonder. Will I need medical attention soon?

"Stop. If you're going to get through this you have to think positive," I remind myself.

***

Energy Awareness & Meditation

I remember there was a time I was unaware of the fact that we are all little balls of energy and our thoughts affect our actions. I didn't know how positive thoughts equal positive actions and so on......

Divine intervention brought me to Intuitive Medium Deborah's group (Deborah Hanlon) meditation in December of 2013. I never listened to the easy listening channel on the radio in the morning, I far preferred my upbeat Techno music, however fate stepped in and had me switch the dial at the precise moment they advertised her meditation event that evening.

Next thing I knew, I was in a hotel conference room of about 45 strangers sitting in the dark and being guided through my first-ever meditation. She gently walked us through visualization and the whole meditation experience. At the point where she walked us through our chakras, I could actually feel my body allowing the positive energy in. Then there was my favorite point where we released all of the negative energy back into the earth. I could actually "see" the blackness exiting my body and going into the ground beneath me, even though my eyes were closed and the room was pitch black! I felt lighter at the end of the session and my shoulders no longer felt like they were touching my ears in heaviness. I went home to tell my husband of my experience and he said "I looked like I was glowing". This was the start of my spiritual journey.

Once you become aware of energy, you can see what patterns exist within your world. I began to notice my energy shift when my husband came into the room. I felt a nervous energy. I felt uneasy. Once you are aware, that light bulb inside goes on and says "hey wait, something is wrong here!" Once the light bulb is turned on you can start to make the necessary changes towards a happier existence.

I went to a few more meditation events hosted by Deborah and then signed up for her Reiki 1 certification class in April, 2014. This class was just what I needed! I further dug deep and uncovered years of hidden negative "tapes" (as Deborah called it) running through my body that affected my daily choices. The tape was recorded during my early years and being replayed over and over, creating my life patterns.

I read numerous books about spirituality, energy awareness, self-help, meditation and Buddha. I even got a Siddartha and Ganesh statue for my room! I committed to daily meditation. I wrote in my journal regularly. I undid my "numbness" that I had for so long and truly became AWARE! I became a master of my mind rather than mastered by my mind (Zen proverb).

It was the start of my "mind training". My ability to use the power of my thoughts to create whatever I desire. You have this same ability. You just need to tap into it and put it to use for yourself.

***

I see a group of volunteers ahead, standing on the sidelines. They're holding large pieces of cardboard out. I watch some of the other racers place their hands on the cardboard and then into their armpits and I realize the cardboard is covered in Vaseline. Yes! As I pass the group holding the cardboard, I stop and wipe my hand across it, and then cover my armpit area where the chaffing was starting to cause bleeding from the motion of my arms going back and forth and rubbing my arm skin against my armpit and side skin. I definitely didn't visualize bloody armpits during my mental training for this race! The Vaseline offers some relief, and I keep going.

I hear music playing loudly up ahead. As the road straightens out I can see a band playing in the yard of some house. There are kids cheering for the racers, and a table with watermelon on it. I stop for a minute. Someone hands me a piece of watermelon and I take a bite. It's like heaven! Cold. Refreshing. Sweet.

I get back on the race route, harder now than it was at the start. I stop for Gatorade and bananas at a few other homes where the people have come out to encourage us to keep going. It is truly a community event and I am so thankful to be part of it all.

I imagine how horrible I must look right now. Dripping in sweat. Exhausted. A far cry from my years of searching for perfection!

***

The Search for Perfection

How does one pass on years of knowledge to their daughter who is graduating from college? My daughter is about to graduate from college and I want to fill her in on all of the years of hardship and life lessons I've experienced to let her know how I got to where I am in life.

To fill her in on the skeletons in my closet so she could have a better understanding of things I did that may not make sense to her. Also, of course, the need to help her NOT make the same choices I did, to find a better path...

I remember being obsessed with perfection. I bit down on a towel in anticipation of the sharp needle that would puncture my shoulder. I sat upright on the coffee table in front of my TV. The needle pierced my skin and the burn started as the serum ran through my veins. Tears entered my eyes. My boyfriend, who had just injected me with steroids looked down upon me as if I had just been initiated into his world. What had I done? Why was I allowing myself to be filled with illegal growth hormones? It was the first and only time I allowed him to "initiate" me into his world but it has long haunted me. Already having had two plastic surgery operations by the time I was 23 years old as well as the obsession to spend 3 hours a day in the gym working out with my personal trainer boyfriend. I looked up to him. He was 16 years older and resembled a Greek God on the outside. So I lived a shallow life of counting every single calorie and recording it in a spiral notebook. Going into a tanning booth and allowing the artificial lightbulbs to brown my skin. Why?

I believe it all comes from my childhood. Insecurity set in at an early age for me. The feelings of not being worthy paved the way for a constant search of approval from others. The need for a father figure allowed an older man to mold me into an image obsessed person who only cared about outwards appearance. It is only now, about twenty years later, that I understand I had to learn these lessons in my teens, twenties and thirties so I could later in life help others.

***

I shake these painful memories from my mind as I approach a sign that says mile marker 18.86. My legs start to seize up and I feel like I can't walk let alone run. I head to the bathroom just across the lawn from the mile marker and sit down on the toilet. Nothing happens. Why can't I go?! I normally pee once an hour! I push and push, but despite all of the water and Gatorade and watermelon I've consumed, I cannot pee.

I go back to the race trail and realize what's happening. My kidneys are shutting down. I knew going into the marathon that this was a possibility. They even warn you on the marathon website and I had to sign a waiver before the race acknowledging that it can happen. All of the people I've seen on the side of the trail being tended to by EMS teams flash into my mind. I could be that person soon. I could be gasping for air, have organs completely shut down, and laying on the side of the road.

No. I came here to finish this race, and I'm going to finish this race. I decide to use my desire to finish to propel me forward. My mind is stronger than my body and I will myself to run. My legs are like wet noodles. I am dehydrated. I am starving. My pace is slow, and not very steady now. But I'm moving. I'm still in the race.

I wipe sweat from my face. It's got to be 85 degrees of pure sun. I stop at every water station to push fluids into my body which had clearly given up. My mind though? My mind refuses to shut down. My mind feels stronger than ever. So I use it to keep going.

I visualize myself crossing the finish line. I pretend to feel the sense of accomplishment I'm sure I'll experience once I cross the finish line. I pretend to hear people cheering for me. I visualize a medal around my neck.

I keep moving. My mind is the only thing keeping me going, so I settle into my thoughts and let it take me forward.

Lorraine K. Toth

Chapter Five

It's amazing how all of my life events have lead me to this moment. Would I even be here if I hadn't gone through an unhappy marriage that ended in divorce? I feel like going through the "stages of divorce" as I call them, helped me grow and finally discover who I really am.

The Stages of Divorce

I won't make this all about divorce, but I think it is important to recognize the stages of grieving and sadness that one goes through in the loss of a significant relationship. Whether that's marriage or a long term relationship, or even the loss of a loved one through death. These are not medical or psychological stages - they are MY explanation and the stages I lived through, and I'm sharing them in case they bring someone comfort as you also move through the stages.

Stage 1 - shock, denial, I can fix this phase
Stage 2 - hot mess, ball of tears, why is this happening to me phase
Stage 3 - anger, I hate him/her phase
Stage 4 - sadness, I am incomplete phase, I long for him/her back
Stage 5 - I can make it through, I kinda like being in charge of me again phase
Stage 6 - so this is living MY way, No one is the boss of me phase
Stage 7 - support systems/friends, so this is what happened to me phase/bonding phase
Stage 8 - lighter existence, I look hot and feel fabulous phase
Stage 9 - acceptance, I realize this happened for a reason phase
Stage 10 - building a new You, healing, I have started over again phase

The Universe Will Light Your Path

So, let's say he leaves you. (Or she does, if you are a man experiencing a divorce or loss of a relationship from your perspective). He moves on way ahead of schedule (the schedule you made up in your head where he pines away about you at home alone for months), and instead - he moves on instantly. You hear of his dates, see it on Facebook, or he tells you the gut wrenching truth.

You will feel a knife is stabbed in your back. Your heart will actually, physically, ache. Your heart will beat so fast and uncontrollably. It sucks, I lived through this so I know firsthand how hard it is.

When my ex came home late one night after a date, back to the home we still shared together as we were separating but not yet divorced, I could actually see and feel the knife in my back just twisting my heart to and fro. It felt like I was being slowly murdered and tortured. I could not shut my mind down from thinking "what was he just doing", "he kissed her", "did he have sex?", "why is his shirt untucked" and on and on. I was completely letting my mind run laps and unable to calm my loudly injured heart. The only thing I could do to turn my mind off that night and stop the tears from falling and relieve the horrific pain was to meditate. I searched YouTube anxiously for a healing meditation. It was exactly what I needed. The meditation guided me through forgiveness, relaxation and put my head into a happier place.

I went from feeling angry at mainly my ex, to feeling gratitude for the "road maps" that were presented to guide me towards letting him go.

Now I will not bullshit you and say this was the end of the road maps or lit tunnels.....

No, no. Since I still loved him and still lived with him while waiting to close on my home, I still waited for the opportunity to sleep/have sex with him. I fantasized about us getting back together. I still desired him and tried my hardest to get his attention. What I did not see at the time was that sex was never our problem, so sex wouldn't get him to "stay" with me.

I also was being blind to the fact that I was giving him the benefit of the doubt that he wasn't having sex elsewhere. I imagined that he couldn't give his body to another just yet, as I couldn't imagine even kissing another man.

Once again, the wonderful universe brightly lit the path for me and showed me in bold print "he is fucking someone else - move on!" Our home iPad, which my son uses, miraculously rebooted and allowed all texts to my ex's phone to come through the iPad so I had to experience once again the heart wrenching knife in my back feeling of betrayal. In fairness to him however, he wasn't betraying me at this point as we were legally separated. I was putting this on myself by not letting go as he clearly did long ago.

I read an amazing quote that I would keep reflecting back on when times like this hit me smack in the face: "Stop trying to pry open doors god shut on purpose for you". I was completely guilty of this.

Once I had the mindset to end this self-inflicted torture and to move on myself, I lost the anxiety of worrying about him. I focused on rebuilding myself. I eliminated the bad things from my head and replaced them with only positive. Meditation was key for keeping my mind on track. I also immersed myself in my art again. Each person is different though, you need to do what will bring **you** relief. While you are in it you will feel like time has stood still and it won't get better. Your heart will ache and you will wonder if you can ever again trust another. You will wonder how you could have let yourself be fooled for so long. These are the wrong thoughts to keep feeding yourself. STOP!!!!

***

Gratitude and Paying It Forward

While I was in midst of the ugly and painful divorce process - I was a huge mess of anxiety and self-doubt. I was not even able to drive to work without bawling on the way. Through divine intervention, Keryl Pesce, a fabulous woman and author of the book "Happy Bitch" came my way. She offered to chat and help me through this tough time as she had also gone through a painful divorce. I was desperate for answers so I took her up on it.

We met halfway between our two homes at a diner truly in East Bumble Fuck, NY and chatted for a couple of hours. Mind you, I was at the stage where I could barely say the word divorce without my eyes welling up in tears, so being in public for the first time discussing this was a huge step forward for me. My friends and family didn't even know at this point. I drove ninety minutes to meet a complete stranger to just talk and hope for wisdom and guidance.

She asked me about what I wanted. It was important for me to look forward, rather than focusing on the past, she said. When I told her I wanted to have someone say "I love you" and mean it, she said she got goose bumps. It wasn't until I said it that I realized how truly sad it was - here I was married for almost 8 years and I really could not remember the last time I heard "I love you" from my husband! I guessed it was three years or more.

This showed me that women are masters of trickery! I kept telling myself this was okay, and while I knew it was not normal or a happy way to live, I accepted it. I was so determined to have the "marriage and family" that I gave up on my own happiness and that urge to feel loved.

Meeting with Keryl allowed me to begin a process of healing. This was also Keryl's way of paying it forward, and she assured me I would do the same for another woman going through divorce someday.

I am now committed to helping other women feel empowerment. I want women to know that you don't have to settle for not feeling loved. Although I think you ultimately need to love yourself first, it is okay to expect and deserve a loving relationship with your spouse.

***

As I allow my mind to wander and remember my struggles, I can appreciate how far I have come in my life. I have seriously come a long way! I look for the mile marker sign. At mile 21 my eyes fill with tears and I start to get very emotional. I choke back a full out sob, and I suppress the urge to cry uncontrollably like I was going for an Oscar performance. I am feeling completely overwhelmed by the emotions flooding through me.

I know at this moment I have made it. I know that no matter what happens in the next few miles, I could at least walk the rest of these 5.2 miles and cross the finish line. But I don't slow down to walk. My body is miraculously continuing to carry me at a run, a slow run, but still, I'm running!

As I get closer to the finish line, I see a bend in the route ahead. I strain to hear what the announcers are saying. Oh! They're announcing the racers names as they cross the finish line?! I can't wait to hear mine. The road straightens out and I'm feeling absolutely energized and stronger than ever. Here I am at the end of 26.2 miles and I'm picking up speed and running an extremely fast pace when I should be collapsing!

I can see the finish line. It's exactly like I visualized it over and over again before the race and even during the race. "Smile, Lorraine!" a photographer takes my picture. I run with all of my heart for the final stretch. The announcer calls my name on the loud speaker as I cross the finish line. Oh my god! I did it! I just ran 26.2 miles. I don't collapse at the finish line like I expected – I feel so completely alive! I'm breathing just fine and I can't even believe the strength I'm feeling.

I look at the picture of me crossing the finish line. Is that me?! I *look* so strong. I look so good for just running five hours in massive sun!

I can do absolutely anything I put my mind to. Finishing this race was all the proof I need to know that this is a *fact.* I hobble to the family area and sit down on the lawn by myself. I sit for a minute, along on the grass, and give myself an inner hug. I watch as other runners cross the finish line. Their families and friends greet them and hug them and offer congratulations.

"Hey! Would you take a picture of me with my finisher medal?" I ask some random stranger. He takes my phone and I pose with my medal for the photo. I walk away and sit down to process what I just accomplished. And while I'm a little jealous and wish I had family and friends to share this experience with, I think I am meant to be here alone. It's so I can tell myself over and over "you can do whatever you desire, Lorraine". I take my phone out and send a text to everyone who said I couldn't do this. I include a photo of me kissing my finisher's medal.

Chapter Six

I sit on the concrete sidewalk, waiting for the shuttle to take me from the race area to my hotel. Everyone else waiting for the shuttles are laughing and talking with each other. I am bursting with pride at what I've just done but there is no one here to share it with – and yet I truly think it's supposed to be this way. I am absorbing this moment of strength just for myself.

At the hotel, I gather my belongings and load up the car. "Holy shit. It's time to get back to regular life already?" I laugh at how strange it is to finish a marathon, to experience all of these emotions, and then to simply jump in the car and return to life like normal.

I drive for a while and then pull over in the parking lot of a car wash. I put my 26.2 sticker on my back windshield. This is the same sticker that I thought years ago was for a radio station and I had no idea what a huge deal it was to be able to post this sticker. I needed to permanently place this sticker on my Mini Copper before driving the four hours home. I can barely walk, I still can't pee, and my only concern is posting this 26.2 sticker on my back windshield! I will never take this sticker off, it will either wear off or I will sell the car. It's a proud "tattoo" that I display.

A while later, I hobble into the Dunkin Donuts, feeling silly because I can barely move. But I wear my "hobble" with pride, too! My running coach told me I would not be able to climb stairs. He said I'd need to either go up them backwards on my butt, or crawl up them for several days later. He was right. I was suddenly so happy I hadn't planned to work for the next four days!

I pull into the driveway of my parent's lake house and struggle to get inside. "Why would you do this to yourself?" my mother asks.

"Was it worth not being able to walk now?" My father says, shaking his head.

I'm shocked. I'm expecting a pat on the back. A "congratulations" for overcoming something I was told I could never do. How did they not grasp the weight of what I just accomplished?!

I sit quietly alone outside, looking at the lake and deciding that this journey was for me, and me alone. I believe I am the only one I needed to prove all of this to – so I wasn't supposed to have a support team. It was my battle alone. I continue to reflect on what got me to this moment.

***

The Part Where You Find Out Who YOU Really Are

For me, finding myself was a rather quick journey. I knew what I enjoyed. I knew what I desired. I therefore put into place what I needed to get to point B from point A.

I rented a cabin on Blue Mountain Lake in the Adirondacks of NY for a long weekend. It was the perfect place to escape the pain of my divorce and the constant reminders of "the us" that used to exist in his house and from seeing the photos of the old "us" in a pile on the floor.

By unplugging from my current reality of a broken home I was able to fix myself and reflect inward. The cabin was a serene piece of heaven for me. The fact that I had no cell or Wi-Fi service and no television forced me to deal with the devil inside. I wrote in my journal and poured out my true feelings. I painted. I read. I slept, finally. I ate when I wanted. I drank a lot of wine!!!

It is scary looking inside. You may see things you do not like about yourself. But there is such acceptance in allowing yourself to be you. Find out what makes you tick. What do you enjoy? So many of us live according to our spouse's set of rules. This is the chance for you to really do what you want! It is so exciting when you think about it that way.

You will be lonely. There were so many times I wanted to call my ex and beg for him to take me back. I longed for him to hold me one last time, to kiss me passionately one more time, to have sex one more time. This was just my mind playing tricks on me since this would not get me to my end result of true happiness. For eight years, I kept my true self at bay since it was not what he needed. I lost the fire inside.

One night alone in my cabin, I began to read pages of my diary that I have kept over the years. Almost every page began with "we are fighting again" or "I am so stressed out". My mind forgot these pages, I tricked myself and only remembered the good times with him. Therefore, I strongly recommend everyone keeps a journal or a diary. While it serves as a great source of past reflection it also is such a tool in purging all of those emotions inside to an unbiased and completely open ear.

***

As the sun sets over the lake, I think about the marathon. Probably the most important lesson I learned with this whole experience is that the body will give up before the mind. I have fully regained my air. I can truly breathe again. Inner, mental strength is so valuable and necessary anytime you decide to push the limits. Prepare your mind first. I did this by visualizing myself crossing the finish line and really FEELING how it would be even before it happened. I conditioned my mind for the outcome I desired. You can, too.

Poetry to release emotion

If you are like me in times of sadness and transition you look to other's words to help you through. You search for an author or story that you relate to, to let you know you are not alone.

My poetry that follows is for that purpose. It was written when my heart was raw. It was cleansing for me to get the words out of my head and to try and convey the emotion on paper.

You may be able to relate to some of my experiences. You may see yourself in the words.

Just know that you are not alone. Somewhere, someone else is experiencing the deep sadness of a lost love. Someone else is struggling with making a tough choice. Someone else is not well. Someone else is filled with hope.

Take what you need from these poems. May they heal, inspire or amuse.

Poetry Contents

5k – Child & Ignorance

10K – Lessons & Ache

13.1K – Love & Loss

15K – Anger & Poison

20K – Raw & Hurt

26.2K - Air & Growth

50K - Win & Inspire

5K

Childhood

&

Ignorance

Safety

You watched and did nothing.

You saw my innocence shattered.

You saw the fear in my eyes and the screams in my throat.

All were silenced in secrecy and shame.

You did nothing to protect me.

So I grew up way too fast and was forced to become my own parent.

I tried to right all of those wrongs.

I tried to bury all of those painful memories.

I tried to re-create a happier childhood.

I tried to build that white picket fence dream I was never allowed to live.

Each feeling of injustice.

Each cry for help never heard.

Each tear shed longing for a better life.

Each bruise upon my skin.

Each drop of blood down my face.

They led me to look for safety in all of the wrong places.

They all led me down a path of trying to
cover-up my previous reality of despair.

Trying to forget and repress.

Trying to repave and rebuild.

Trying to heal and be set free.

Not until I learned to confront these
demons of the past,

did I learn I was meant to save myself all
alone.

Fear

Lock the door.

Hide in the corner.

Feel your heart pound.

Feel your stomach uneasy.

Your ears are on high alert.

Fear is around the corner.

This is not your first battle with it.
Oh poor child,

I am sorry this will not be your last.

How many harsh words will your ears be
forced to hear?
How many bruises upon your skin will you
see?
How many tears of sadness will flow from
your eyes?

How many my dear,

before you decide to no longer let fear
enter your door?

Lifeless

Protect your heart sweet young girl.

Learn the lesson early on,

that some will try to steel the blood that makes it beat.

Learn that only you can shield it from the trauma that can be inflicted upon it.

Some will promise to be your Prince.

Some will promise to honor it.

Some will momentarily carry it's responsibility.

Oh sweet girl, just know…

this is not their duty.

It is yours.

For giving them the power over your heart,

will only leave you feeling lifeless.

My Child

You grab a hold of my thumb

and wrap your tiny fingers around mine.

All my worries washed away

with your innocent touch.

Any stress or sadness in my world,

is no match for your unconditional love.

To hold you in my arms now,

to know I had the honor of carrying you
internally for nine months.

Simply stated - for you to be my child.

This is my life's purpose.

Anytime I feel sorrow creep in,

all I need is a hug from you and
perspective is granted.

For there is no greater gift,

than your love.

Whispers

Take my hand,

I've got you.

Take my heart,

I'll beat for you.

I longed for you to say these to me.
I waited patiently.

Things we long to hear from another

that we should be saying to ourselves.

If you expect to hear words whispered from
someone when you do not say them to
yourself, you give them the power over
your soul.

They can take it away.

They can never say those words.

Whisper to yourself sweet darling.
Take your own hand.

You will grow like an oak tree in a forest
of unknowns.

You will see that no matter the storms you
face,

that you will remain standing.

Paint

Screams of terror never voiced,

come out as art through your paintings.

You tremble when he is near

and shut yourself in your bedroom.
This is your escape.

Inside your bubble of art,

you paint the life you long for.

It is a beautiful and loving home,

filled with the kind words you long to
hear.

Support, encouragement and honesty,

lift you up and out of bed each day with a
smile on your face.

As your paintbrush falls to the floor,

from the slamming of the front door,
reality sets in.

His footsteps come closer.

You wish to be living within your
painting,

this glorious white picket fence dream.

But all of the paint on the canvas,

can not protect you from the hell down the
hall.

Exterior

You see only the exterior,

you see the red lips,

you see the blonde hair,

you see the winged eyeliner

and the curvy body.

What you don't see is the internal bruises

that have been stacked up on top of one
another.

Years of bricks that were built around my
heart for protection.

Years of lessons that boarded up my soul
to block anymore pain from entering.

What you don't see is someone who fought
many battles over the years defending her
worth, her safety, her dreams.

What you don't see is the wisdom that can
only come from having crawled through
hell.

The knowledge of what it feels like to be
burnt, cut up into pieces and then spit
out.

So you can see choose to see the exterior,
the surface image of beauty that exists
only to the plain eye.

Just know that the stained glass pieces
that glow from within are far more
beautiful than any curve on my body or
lash upon my face.

Should I invite you in to take a peek,
would you run away or accept me as I am?

The exterior shall one-day fade.

However, the interior will only continue
to blossom and shine.

Needle

I clench down on a terrycloth towel,

my teeth sink into it's woven fabric.

Cries of pain are silently smothered in
the layers of it's crisp cloth.

The venom courses through my veins.

The piercing of the needle that punctured
my shoulder, has quickly made it's way
down to my heart.

I accepted this torture disguised as a way
to add strength.

I accepted your words that this was
normal.

I looked to you for guidance,

not knowing everything was artificial and
a veil of lies.

So as you shove this needle into my virgin
skin,

I wonder if you felt my innocence creep
out through my pores?

Did you feel the struggle to please you
battle with my questioning conscience?

Did you feel my soul cry out and beg you
to stop?

Did you see the tear of sadness run down
my cheek?

What you said would make me stronger,

has only made me crumble to the ground
like a coward.

Perfection

A glance in the mirror and

thoughts of uncertainty set in.

For you a reflection from it's glass does
not register the reality of what is
actually there.

Instead you just see what needs to be
fixed.

Visions of a scalpel cutting away parts of
you.

Thoughts of a surgeon reshaping your hips,

particles of cellulite sucked away dance
in your head.

So reshape your body sweet girl.

Contour the exterior for the world to see.

You will still always fall short of
perfection-

for without changing the inside,

the outside will never make you happy.

10K
Lessons
&
Ache

Lorraine K. Toth

Roots

The roots go deep.

They do not want to let go.

Woven into one another,

clinging onto hope.
They long to stay buried.

One by one they release.

Some easily break free.

Some need to be cut loose.

Some long to remain covered and hidden.

After much struggle, the old tree is
lifted out.

Only a hole now remains.

The sand begins to cave and fill in the
shallow hole.

A new tree is planted.

The new tree must accept the roots that
remained in it's spot.

It begins to grow around the old wise
roots.

It establishes itself amongst their
history.

Day by day the new tree becomes stronger.

The elements test the new tree's strength.

The tree knows it's destiny so it fights back.

Then one day, it blossoms.

Beauty sprouts out of it. It is a source of inspiration.

It is a new beginning amongst the old.

Puzzle

Sweet girl,

when the pieces of the puzzle do not match up...

Do not doubt yourself.

Do not think you approached the puzzle incorrectly.

Do not question your intelligence.

Leave that puzzle.

Find a new one to assemble.

That one is too broken you see,

no one can put it together.

Not even itself.

Pain

Should I choose not to obey,
you show up unannounced to pay a dreadful
visit.

My head aches, my back seizes up, my knee
throbs.

You throw a right hook to my ribs so I
listen to you.

My ears try to tune into your subtle
hints.

I promise to take better care.

I promise to listen to your warning signs.

However, these are just promises that I do
not obey.

So once again my body cries out.
Listen to me.

You are unhappy.
You are being taken advantage of.
You are living on the fence.

He does not love you.
This is not your life you are living.

The lack of breath in my lungs tells me to
take deeper breaths.

The bags under my eyes tell me to sleep
and slow down.

Your warning I heed not.
I think I can outsmart you.

The pain resurfaces stronger this time.

I fall to the ground and cry out "why
me?".

You answer "I tried to warn you and you
didn't listen."

Ghost

In like a steamy romance novel,
you lit my world on fire.

I still remember when you grabbed my hand

and strolled proudly down the street.

You pulled the car over on the side of the
road just to kiss me,

unable to wait until we parked the car
moments ahead.

We couldn't keep our hands off one
another.
That first night we met.
It was as if we had known each other for
years instead of hours.

Our souls connected that night.
You said I could be your girl.

Then, you disappeared like Houdini.
Gone in a flash with no warning.

Where did you go my ghost?

How does one disappear from such an
amazing first date?

Perhaps you knew of our fate.

Speed Bumps

The ones who come into your life
unexpectedly.

You know they are wrong for you.

They fill a void.

They provide fun and excitement.

You know they are not long term.

But they play an important role,

they help you go back to the correct path.

They help you avoid a decision you regret.

They detour you.

They are your life's speed bump.

Thank them after it is over.

For even though they were not a long term
part of your life, they helped your story
become greater.

This time

This time I will know better.

This time I will see the red flags.

This time I will protect my heart.

The funny thing is I said it all to myself

before we even began.

One gaze into your eyes and any hope of

self protection tossed aside.

A heed of caution had no chance against
our intense chemistry.

Words of wisdom no match for the way we
effortlessly fit.

Lessons learned prior left unspoken when
our eyes met.

You tell yourself to be careful.

You tell yourself you deserve better.

You tell yourself stay away, this one will
burn you.

What you forget to tell yourself is that
love is deaf.

Wait

Just give it time they say,

if it is meant to be he will come back.

Days pass.

I await our reunion.
The lock remains on my heart,

with only you holding the key.

How long should I wait?

How long shall I turn others away?

Months pass.
Sorrow still clouds my soul.

Then one day I realize,

were you ever really even worth the wait?

Excuses

By the second time of excuses,

it's your fault to stay for a third.

Leave.

I know. I stayed.

I can no longer even tally up the number.

The excuses that my ears innocently
listened to,

fell too often from your lips.

So what is my excuse for staying?

Rain

Each drop hits the roof,
I hear it pound upon the shingles.

It reminds me of the tears,
that fell from my eyes after you left.
They fall and hit the paper I write upon.

They splatter on the words of sorrow.

They hit the letters but alike the rain in
the sky, it does not end.

The thunder and clouds fill the sky.
The forecast is ominous.

Is rain not supposed to cleanse?
Is rain not what makes the grass grow?

If so please cleanse my heart of your
memories.

Please allow my heart to flourish without
you.

Rain - allow my field of happiness to grow
once again,

allow my heart to blossom with each
blessed drop.

Allow me to thrive in a new environment
void of you.

Paths

Some paths unfold through careful consideration.

Some appear out of nowhere and rock your world.

Some leave you breathless in anticipation.

Some leave you gasping for air and writhing on the floor in pain.

You will be given many signs from above,

many roads to choose from.

Let the universe be your guide, your map, your clues.

Listen in and choose wisely my dear,

as some paths are simply not meant for you.

Island

It will be too late.

So go ahead and tell yourself that you
just need time.

Tell yourself that you need to calm the
stormy seas before you make way to my
island.

Stall the decision you know is right.

Cope with the sadness by popping open
another bottle of beer.

Smoke away the sorrow.
Do as you need.

Then, when you realize I was meant for
you…

When you realize I adored you completely.

When you realize how we fit perfectly.

When you realize I was the drug that kept
you calm.

When you crave my touch upon your body and
soul.

Try to come back to my island of solace.

Try to come back into my life.

Try to be the man you should have been
months before but were too weak.

It will be too late.
I will have moved on.

My island will be better suited to protect
against those with no intentions of
staying forever.

My island will be healed from you finally.

You will miss me and know you made the
mistake of a lifetime.

You will try to get me back as your lady

but it will be too late my darling.

Voice

Break my heart and out falls paintings and poems.

You came into my life to once again challenge my soul.

For with you turning my world upside down, the faucet of creativity flows.

I cursed you at first.

I wanted to forget our romantic moments that replay in my head.

Then I let the ache of lost love inspire.

The visions of us in the past dancing in my head now make art.

The words we said, the looks we gave, the memories we made - they now live on as I finally write.

I write to help others thrown the curve ball just when they thought they won the game.

For the ones who believed their search was over.

For the ones who thought it couldn't get
better and then it came crashing down.

Your lack of words I longed to hear,
became songs for all of the broken
hearted.

I now know I was meant to be a voice for
them.

Thank you for my voice.

Cocoon

I'm going into a cocoon.

When I emerge I will be cleansed of your memories.

I will fly away a weightless Butterfly,

in search of a healthy new love to land upon.

One that is able to thrive and flourish,

instead of stalling growth.

I should have never considered landing upon you,

I should have seen it would never be reciprocal.

I should have not crawled as the loving caterpillar upon your leaf.

For you never had any intention for us of a future blossoming.

Coward

Refuse to stand up for yourself.
Then throw me into the toxic mix.

Sprinkle in some empty promises,
avoid truths.

Live on a fence where no decision is made,
this coward you became.

You think you can have the best of both
worlds.
You believe you can have your cake and eat
it too.

Tell me, does it feel good to stand in the
middle?
What happens when both sides leave, can
you stand on your own?

I will not be around to find out the
answer.

13.1K

Love

&

Loss

Unlocked

For so long it was dark.
Hopeless and untouched.

You came in and lit it up,

warm and glowing,

softer and sweeter.

The beat was resuscitated.

The blood pumping once again.

The hope restored.

The holes repaired.

Thank you.

Sincerely,

My Heart

Heart

I should be angry with you.

I should curse the day our paths crossed.

I should resent you for accepting all of
my kindness.

I should begrudge you for the precious
time I put my heart aside for you.

For you see my darling, I put my heart on
a shelf.

There it sat and sat waiting for you to
pick it up.

Time went by and it collected dust as you
never reached up.

It waited patiently for you to take it
into your arms.

For you to have the courage to call it
yours.

So much love to give. Yet, all it did was
sit on this shelf alone.

For you did not have the courage.

Or perhaps you knew you were not worthy?

Worthy of such a gift -
this gift of my heart.

So instead of anger towards you,
I only feel pity.

Palette

I write to rid myself of words I long to
say to you.

I write and paint to cleanse myself of the
emotions attached to your memory.

Those kisses I long to lay upon your lips,

the embrace I long to never let go of.

The touch I long to rest my fingers upon
your face,

the gaze I long to reflect in your eyes.

The smell of you I long to inhale,

the taste of you I long to swallow.

So I paint and write to release these
pains of losing you.

Each stroke of the brush releases longing
and sadness.

Each dip into the palette brings hope of
repairing my heart.

The palette which is at first empty
symbolizing how I feel without you,

becomes filled with color, life and
beauty.

So while you left me void, wilted and
hurt,

I thank you for the inspiration to create
once again.

Ideal

I envision the perfect mate.

I dream up the details of his look.

I imagine his touch upon my body.

I fantasize what it would feel like to be
his girl.

Every time I dream this dream of my ideal,
I dream of you.

Hidden

I know better.

Yet I can not stop.

So, in secrecy we meet.

In darkness we become one.

If only for a moment,

a taste to satisfy the urges,

it is better than nothing.

A source of pleasure in your life,

a ray of sunshine in your gloomy existence

that will never see the light of day.

Fire

We knew two fire signs would bring roaring
flames.

We knew it would be the heat of the flames
to ignite intense passion.

With that intensity comes the knowledge
the fire will go out.

The fire did not go out slowly though.

It did not simmer to grey smoky ashes.

You put it out abruptly.

The flames were smothered and air flow cut
off.

Only ashes remain.

The grey coals represent the cherished
memories of the beautiful fire that once
burned bright.

The feeling of the heat that once warmed
my soul has been replaced with a dull
ache.

I ask myself if I should have walked into
that fire.

I would have saved myself from being
burnt.

But I also would have never felt your
heat.

Dull the Pain

The wine reminds me of our gourmet dinners
at home.

The scotch reminds me of our jazz club
evenings out.

The tequila reminds me of the country
concerts we watched.

The beer reminds me of the nights at the
slots.

I long for a drink to just be a drink.

I long for the drink to just be a vice.

I long for them to be a cover-up, an
escape.

I long for them to dull the pain.

Memories of you live in all of these
things,

flashbacks of the past unwilling to fade.

Release your hold upon my heart,

so I can drown in sorrow.

Release your hold upon my soul,

so I can be numb.

Release your chains upon my emotions,

so a beverage can once again quench my
thirst

instead of reminding me of the sweetness

that once touched my lips.

Dance

Breathless in anticipation.
One touch from you ignites a fire within.
Up against a wall,

your body connects with mine.

I accept you fully.

We become one.

This dance of passion and pleasure
consumes me.

One more deep kiss,

one more longing embrace,

one more moment to feel our naked body's
heat converge,

one more time to collapse together in
ecstasy.

My heart beats fast, my body ready to
receive you.

Dance this dance with me. Just one more
dance of passion.

Let the drips of sweat coat our dance
floor,

let the beating of our hearts be our
music,

let the smell of us blended be the candle
that burns,

let this song never end.

Drug

Some are meant to come into your life with
no warning.

The ones who an instant and unexplained
pull draws you in.

The chemical attraction, the desire, the
admiration.

It becomes a drug you can not live
without.

The need to be with them overtakes reason.

You know you need to escape for safety of
your heart, but the addiction to them
wins.

So your longing becomes stronger with each
day, each kiss.

Needing more and more to fill the void.

Then one day your drug disappears

and you lie on the ground alone in tears.

Nothing replaces them, though you try.

How could someone be so powerful?

To make you feel like you are on top of a
mountain and then with no warning - buried
alive?

These ones who draw you in like a moth to
a flame.

Do they know they will burn you with their
heat?

Do they know you will collapse when the
needle of love is withdrawn?

Crave

My body aches for you…

your touch,

your kiss,

your smell,

your taste.
You are an addiction I can not quit.

I count the days until

I can once again consume you - my drug.

Until I can once again inject the needle
of desire and unleash the pent up longing
for you, for us.

I count the minutes…

my body wet in anticipation.

My heart beats faster,

my nectar flows ready to accept you in.

You enter the room,
I long for you to consume me.

Just one more time.

I need a fix.

Stop the craving.

Lust

Pinned up against the wall, hands
overhead.

Leaning over the kitchen counter,

Straddled in the chair,

then mounting on the couch.

Clothes thrown everywhere.

Pillows tossed and sheets un-tucked.

From the moment you enter my home,

desire can not be contained.

In any possible way,

any location,

any position,

I am yours to be taken.

All too quickly it comes to an end.

Your time has suddenly expired and you
must flee.

Back to your other life, back to your
charade.

The smell of passion lingers after you
leave.

I always wish I had savored the moment
more in your absence.

What I should be wishing is that you never
left.

Ache

The ache washes over me.

The tear forms in my eye.

My heart, it feels punctured.

My soul, it feels lost.

I gasp for air.

I tell myself it will be ok.

Deep breaths are forced.

Day by day I tell myself.

I try to forget you.

I try to move on.
I search for happier thoughts.

I tell myself it wasn't meant to be.

If only I could believe that.

So, I sit in silence.

The pain comes and goes.

It will unfold as it should.

My heart will heal. We will move on.

What we were will always be missed.

So wouldn't it have been easier had we
never even kissed?

Reminders

I sigh to let air in.

I sigh to let thoughts of you escape.

I try to erase your memory.

The touch you burnt into my mind.

Post it notes hang throughout my home,

reaffirming reminders to attract in a
healthy and steady relationship.

They state daily for me to remain strong
and what is meant to be will come into my
path.

They remind me love will come my way.

It would have all been so much easier,

if you had just decided to stay.

New Chapters

Just one more time we tell ourselves.

Just one more tender kiss.

Just one more passionate embrace.

What lasts only minutes however,

tears at my soul for months.

Each time we step back into our burning
fire,

makes it that much harder to be left out
in the cold.

We know better than open a book we closed.

Do we hope for a new ending with the same
words inside?

Do I hope for a new chapter to appear

where you are truly my Prince?

Do you hope to make peace with yourself

existing in a story that has no happy
ending?

While you have paused our story and begun
a new book,

I am here waiting in the middle of a
sentence

and longing for a sequel.

Today

Today I shed my first tear over you.

It ran down my face like a freight train.

The sadness overtook me.

The memories of you rushing in and
unstoppable.

I gasped for air.

Emotions crept in. With no warning they
knocked at my door.

I decided to let them enter.

The tears although unwelcome visitors,
have offered relief.

With each tear I shed, a key is turned.

Today I still hope you are the one to turn
that key.

Today I let the tears remind me of my love
for you.

In each crystal clear tear is hope you
wipe my face dry of sadness someday.

Mine

Some aren't meant to be possessed.
Some are meant to roam free and wander.

I try to lasso your heart,
the rope falls short.

I try to cast a spell upon your soul,
the magic dissipates into thin air.

Why is it we want the ones we can not
have?

Why do we torture ourselves with hopes of
a future

with those incapable of commitment?

Why do we say maybe he will change his
mind,

when we shouldn't want those needing
convincing?

Isn't it far easier to admit -

you were never meant to be mine.

Storm

Your lips I crave,

your touch I long for.

In a short amount of time,

the impact immeasurable.

You came in like a gentle breeze,

leaving my hair standing on end

and my skin softly caressed.

You went out like a tsunami,

leaving my eyes gushing with tears

and my heart broken into scattered pieces.

Did I not see the forecast of fate?
Did I ignore the weather's warning signs?

Surely I could have avoided your storm.

Surely I could have seen those ominous
clouds overhead.

My heart could have sought shelter.

My soul could have been boarded up for
safety.

Now I must rebuild,

what the wake of you tore down.

Box

I saw you from across the room
and I felt my heart leave my body.

Your eyes met mine and I knew,
it was beyond my control.

You were the gift I had asked for.
Delivered to me through fate.

The unexplained pull.
The magnetic force of us.

The hunger to dive in deeper, to develop
our relationship faster.

This caused me to ignore your red flags
and hazard signs.

The words "Caution" screamed out from
above,

but I ignored every single warning.

For when our lips met I lost all sense of
reason.

Years of lessons forgotten.

Wisdom out ruled.

There was no sweeter kiss.

No more passionate embrace.

You were irresistible.

You were a source of pleasure.

You were the perfectly wrapped gift on the outside,

a present I longed for and wanted to cherish.

However, once I opened this beautiful offering,

you stabbed me deep through the heart.

Now I know,

I should have left that bow on to keep your box sealed shut.

Merry Go Round

Just one more time,

one more ride -

for old times sake.

I pay the price to get on,

each time my heart allows you in again.

One more thrill,

one more jaunt through ecstasy,

one more chance to savor your lips upon
mine.

Nine months now -

of me saying "One more time".

The ups and downs,

this ride to nowhere -

just going in circles.

Still, I can not get off.

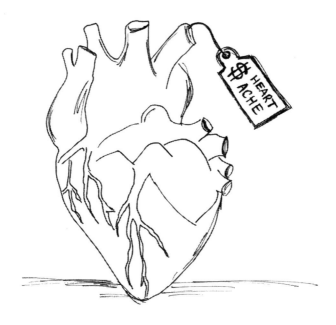

Muse

You are a knife in my heart that bleeds
poetry.

Like the moth to a flame,

the outcome is ominous

but the draw irresistible.

My muse that comes with

the hefty price-tag of heartache.

These powerful words vomited to expunge
love lost.

I only hope they help others who ache,

others who are filled with so much longing

that poems dance in their heads

to convey the songs in their hearts.

Space

"Space is relative",
this is what you say when I ask for you
to make room for me in your life.

Well then, notice the distant and dark
space where I am no longer there to love
you.

Notice the space in your arms where I used
to nestle in.

Notice the space on your fingertips where
we used to walk hand in hand through town.

Notice the space on your head where I used
to run my fingers through your hair.

Notice the space on your lips where I used
to passionately kiss you.

But most of all —

Notice the way you feel when you know
another occupies the spot by my side you
carelessly left vacant.

Maybe then you will notice the lonely and
sad space in your heart crying out.

Maybe then you will truly understand
space.

15K
Anger
&
Poison

Jekyll & Hyde

I would carefully enter our home.
Tiptoeing through the front door.

Un-aware of what version of you may greet
me today.

I would look for the signs,

if you were smiling I knew we would make
love and

have a fun night.

If you were silent and seemed anxious,

I knew affection would be withheld.

This is how you punished me.

For when I did not behave according to
your plan,

you withdrew your needle of affection.

Venom

I look back and wonder,

how I endured your toxicity for so long.

Then I realize, I didn't.

It seeped into my pores.

It made me ill.

It made me shut down emotionally.

It took away my breath.

Until I withdrew that needle of your
venom,

the symptoms of living in a loveless

marriage would continue to poison my

body and soul.

Obey

Spew your venom.

Paint your picture.

Make yourself the victim.

She will see for herself one day,
that it was you, not I.

She will see when you do the same to her—
for failing to be the vision that suits
your reality.
For not being your eager project.
For not obeying your commands.

Distractions

Sling your hateful words my way, they will
bounce off my skin.

Taint my reputation with the twisted and
dark version of me that you have painted
for others.

Replace me in seconds with your next
project that you will skillfully mold.

Cover up any memories with an instant
rebound to dull any feelings of lost love.

Divert your soul with glasses of Rum over
ice to ease the discomfort of my memory.

Distractions.

Diversions.

Avoidance.

Call it what you desire.

Then, do as you wish for it no longer is
my concern you see.

I dealt with the death of our
relationship.

I met those demons head on.

I mourned and I buried "us".

I chose not to distract.

Now I wonder, when your band-aid falls off
will you bleed?

Or has your heart become black and numb
with no blood at all?

Still Standing

Thank you for being the asshole.

The dark twisted soul that spewed
blackness.

Thank you for always knocking me down,
and never lending a hand to get back up.

As I stand here now,
I have such a clear perspective.

I have air.
I am reborn.
I am thriving.

But you just remain an asshole.

Teacher

Oh teacher the lessons you lay down before
me I am not ready to yet learn.

The heartache you present to me I am not
ready to yet open.

The tears you release I am not ready to
yet wipe dry.

The clouds in the sky you place overhead I
am not yet ready to fill with sun.

Your lessons while necessary for my path,
come with no warning and leave me
paralyzed.

Just as I begin to feel strong enough to
stand and walk,

you knock me back down to teach me I must
first crawl.

Oh teacher I beg of you to be gentle and
kind,

for don't you see that love is blind?

20K
Raw
&
Hurt

Window

Look through the panes of glass

and see my intense sadness and sorrow.

The layers of glass to withstand storms.

The seal that wraps around to keep out the
unwanted.

The shade can be drawn to block what
should not be seen.

Pull the curtains when it is too much to
bare.

Pretend your view was never there.

Specks of dirt and dust begin to cloud my
view,

but I will still look out my window in
search of you.

River

My throat is raw with hurt.

My eyes swollen shut from tears.

When will this river of emotions stop
flowing?

When will the sun shine overhead again?

I know the painful answer.

Not until I let you go.

Lorraine K. Toth

Thief

My heart was pure,
it was ready for you.

Ready to give you the abundant warmth you
needed.

However, your heart was black.
Dark.
Far too cold.

With no space for me to enter.

So instead you swallowed all of my love,
sucked up my heat,
stole my breath
and left me frozen and lifeless.

You cowardly thief.
You took with no intention of
ever giving back.

You robbed me of my love.

Fool

I knew if I waited for you to be mine,
I would be a considered a fool.

An imbecile.

You begged me for patience.
You wished for more time.
So like a fool, I gave you the precious gift of more.

I took the chance of looking foolish in hopes of feeling your love.

I waited for you to make room for me in your kingdom.

I sat there longing for you to make me your Queen.
But you never came for me.

I sat a distraught Princess filled with tears.

I sat in an empty castle,
I remained a lonely fool.

You should have slain me,
rather than have me sit in
silence waiting.

Death would have been easier.

Extinction more peaceful than the
truth that you never intended
to have our kingdoms unite.

Senses

Go away - I say to the thoughts of you
that flutter into my mind upon awakening.

Hide - I say to the random things like
toothpaste that remind me of you around my
home.

Stop playing - I say to the song we used
to dance to in the kitchen.

Change the recipe - I say to the flavor of
the dessert we used to feed one another by
spoonfuls.

Turn it off - I say to the movie we
watched together while you fell asleep on
my chest.

Put it out - I say to the smell of the
fire that makes me reminisce of our nights
drinking wine in front of it.

Rip them off - I say to the feel of the
black satin sheets on the bed we used to
make love in.

I try to run from the memories of you.

To run from these overwhelming and
powerful moments of "us".

Take away my senses.
For each bares too many painful thoughts
of you and I.

Words

You are a double edged sword.

After you leave, my heart bleeds sadness
onto these pages that create art.

Words of love lost transform into

passionate poetry.

Yet the pain of not having you by my side,

still poisons my soul.

Extraordinary

You tell yourself you no longer miss me.

You tell yourself you are happy.

Why then do you clench your jaw?

Why then do you bite your nails?

Why then does your shoulder ache and your
neck lock up?

Why then is your stomach in knots?

Could it be you realize you left the
extraordinary?

You left bliss for the refuge of the norm.

You left the bubbles of anticipation,

for the safety of routine and criticism
your ears accustomed to.

Tell me, is it worth popping that pill to
dull the pain of regret?

Is it worth the internal struggle of
feeling your body craving my touch?

Is it worth the shallow grave you dug
yourself into for settling?

If it is the feeling of shelter you seek,
you have built your home on the wrong
sand.

Wouldn't life better lived touching the
sky because you are high on love rather
than buried alive?

Broken

Why do I torture myself with photos of us?
Why do I reminisce about the nights in
your arms?

Why do I listen to the songs we danced to?

Each thought or image of you brings a
knife to my heart.

I try to wipe away the sadness in my mind
that runs over and over like a broken
record.

I say to myself to give it time, you will
fade from memory.

I debate trying to replace you with a
distraction of another.

However, I know what we were can not be
replaced.
So I sit alone and ponder are you doing
the same?
Have you moved on?
Do you miss us?

The lack of communication only makes it
that much harder.
The silence deafening.

My mind makes up stories.

My heart longs for a happy ending,

with us reunited.

How

How could you allow me to adore you?

How could you keep me prisoner to your
lies?

How could you let it go on for so long?

You knew you had nothing to give in
return.

You knew you would not stay.

You knew it would not evolve.

You just took and took.

I was so honest and upfront.
You knew my intentions.

I was painfully in love with you.

How could you just throw that all away?

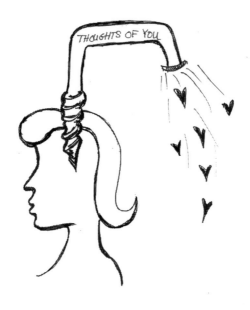

Hose

I want to drill a hole in my head,

so I can spill out these thoughts of you.

I want to hose it down,

to cleanse myself of your memory.

Then, when you are washed away -

I can repave my road to happiness.

Lorraine K. Toth

Knife

"How could you?" I ask repeatedly.

You swore there would be no broken hearts,
you swore no one would get hurt.

The joy in our routine, the comfort in
your arms, the surrender to your lips.

All a distant flicker of what once was the
norm and is now a knife deep in my soul.

I believed in your words.

I believed in that loving look in your
eyes.

I believed in how you held me tightly.

I believed in us.

You swore we would always be friends.

So why do I sit here alone,
why does this feel like the end?

Need

I know I need to get angry.

I need to say "Fuck you"!

I need to drain the sorrow,

and turn it into detestation.

You were a wrecking ball to my world,

and a knife in my heart.

Still,

I only feel love for you.

Leave

Actions -

I waited for them.

Promises -

empty words from you.

Foolish -

to have waited so long for you to change.

Hurt -

you took and left me broken hearted.

Wise -

enough now to know I was too good for you.

Leave -

what I will say if you try to come back to
me.

26.2K
Air
&
Growth

Forward

When each breath fills me with hope
and every footstep forward brings me
happiness.

I will then know I am over you.

Run

With each foot forward I create a new me.

With each touch of my heel on the ground,
my soul begins to rebuild.

The wall you built,
the hateful words you slung my way,
one by one they fall to the ground
and are absorbed by the earth.

They no longer affect me and warm light
shines in.

Buds of new life and hope blossom.

I run filled with newly cleansed air.

My pace quicker having set the burden of
you free.

I run to prove I am still alive without
you.

You thought you could take my air and I
would fade away.

You thought your words would tear me down
and cripple me.

You thought I would wither away like a
dying flower.

So I run to show you I made it.

I run towards a happy ending you can never
touch.

I run so you see you did not break me.

I run towards a new me.

Finish Line

My legs did not carry me across that
finish line,

my heart and soul did.

All those times I hid in fear,

all those moments I was betrayed,

all those years I needed your love,

all the times you hit instead of hugged.

They filled my lungs with air,

the air of a survivor.

One who had the mind of a champion,

rather than the martyr and abused.

50K

Win

&

Inspire

Artist

We see beyond just a flower or sunrise.
We see beyond color.
We see beyond shape.

Paintings are our souls purging.
Poetry is our sadness vomited.
Photos are our view of beauty.

So when you criticize an artist -
when you ask us to be more responsible,
when you ask us to stop daydreaming,
when you ask us to be more normal,
just know you are asking us to die.

For the fountain of creativity,
is the blood cursing through our
artistic veins.

Empire

You worry of the fear of falling.

I revel in the joy of flying.

I stand on the edge.

Knowing darkness exists below,
but only focusing on the light above.

Yes, my foot can stumble.

Yes, I may bleed.

Yes, I can lose my breath.

But I feel so alive,
This is my moment.

The air fills my lungs
and passion forces expansion.

I will not back down.
I will not retreat.

Welcome to my Empire.

Lorraine K. Toth

Entrepreneur

I'd rather build something where nothing
once stood.

I'd rather fall on my face trying,

than be chained to a desk eight hours a
day.

I'd rather the uncertainty of making the
rent,

than the dull routine that comes with a
weekly paycheck.

You can call me hasty, ludicrous and just
plain mad.

However, you will never call me
predictable and boring.

The excitement of creating new dreams,
tastes, sights and sounds.

The nights of not being able to fall
asleep as my mind runs wild.

The heart beating from seeing my logo go
up on the wall,

displaying what was once only a vision and
now symbolizing my brand.

The chance to answer that question "What
do you do?" with a bubbling voice only a
proud entrepreneur would reverberate.

So you can criticize my leaps of faith, my
risks, my failures, my should have knowns,
my financial losses.

"But at least I tried", will be my reply
over and over.

At least I did not slowly wither away
during an eight-hour daily sentence in a
cubicle.

At least I lived.

Lorraine K. Toth

Epilogue

When I began writing this book three years ago I gave a copy to a friend who was also an author and in my Reiki certification classes. He said that the book was good but there was no happy ending, no message, no conclusion, no lesson. It was unfinished. I agreed with him so I put the book on the back burner and continued to live my life mindfully aware and present. I let the lessons come pouring in over the next few years. At the time I began writing I was completely raw with hurt, sorrow and disappointment. I was broken open. I wrote as a release of the pain. I wrote with the intention of helping others going through the hell that I felt I was in.

The last three years taught me more than I could have ever imagined. I am in a completely different space now. I am healed. I am happy. I no longer need someone to fill the gap. I am enough. The pain, anxiety and self-doubt have turned into confidence, inner peace and amazing energy that I radiate outward.

From a romantic/relationship standpoint - I am now at a stable place of complete happiness and being open to allow for this happy ending my friend had mentioned. I know this to be truth as the universe in all of its wondrous glory gave me a sign that I am ready. Two hearts appeared in my path. This is the first time I was given a sign of TWO hearts, mind you. It had only been an individual heart shape prior that I would see. (I spoke of these signs earlier in the book but basically, I would see a heart shape on the road in squished gum or a heart shape in my cracked egg shell, etc.) It is not a coincidence to me that I had this pair of hearts appear the day after I finally said the words I had been longing to say for years – "boyfriend".

After the divorce I longed to fill the void with a significant other. What I did not realize until recently was that I was not ready for a boyfriend, therefore I had to wait. I had to walk my path, complete my process. I went through countless "wrong turns" and kissed a lot of frogs before I finally found my prince. Each day now I am filled with gratitude for waiting and not settling. To know that something so magical and "perfect for me" is possible made the long wait worth it.

All of those lonely nights on the couch with a movie and popcorn, all of those horrible first Tinder dates where I wanted to run out within seconds of saying "Hi", all of those boys I went on a few dates with and would always go home disappointed, all of those other couples I would look at longingly....it was all worth it because now I have what I wanted.

Even with the years of "misery", I would not change a thing. It all led me to what I have now. A relationship where I feel content and at peace. A partner that I had been searching for that makes me want to be a better person and vice versa. Someone I do not want to change a thing on. Someone who I actually bubble with joy every time I see him. Through my lessons in energy awareness I always reflect inwards and ask myself - "how does it feel"? With this person, it always feels amazing!

If I can encourage you to be patient.... please do. I know it is hard. I know that it feels like forever when you are in it. The holding pattern is there for a reason though. Just know that the universe has a far better plan for us than we imagined. There is a purpose to waiting. My purpose was so I healed 100% from my divorce. So I did not repeat old patterns that no longer served me. So that I did not settle with someone who was truly not a match for me.

Therefore, to you who may be reading this as you are just getting out of a divorce, or to you who has been on the dating scene for years and is frustrated with all the Mr. Wrongs or to you who has been lonely and depressed because you sit on the couch alone with Netflix....I feel you. I was you.

This time where you are being forced to wait is for you own good. It makes you reflect on what you DO want so that when you get it, you appreciate it. Allow the Universe to do its work at the pace necessary. Realize there will be lessons along the way. Then, when you get what you have asked for express the gratitude in your heart for it all coming together better than you could have planned yourself.

Update on the epilogue:

So I was recently sent a teacher in between the time I wrote my epilogue and the time I got ready to finally publish this book. A teacher is a lesson, something thrown into your path to educate you. It is then up to you to either fight the lesson or to accept it with grace. I chose to accept my "teacher" and turn the sadness, frustration and loss into actually printing this book.

The teacher taught me that I have a voice inside me that can help others going through similar situations. The teacher taught me that I am capable of love. The teacher taught me that I need to be more in tune with what I allow to come into my life. One bad decision can cause quite the domino effect. The teacher was necessary for me to re-affirm what I deserve. Right before I made my decision to end the unhealthy relationship I was once again faced with "illness" signs within my body. My shoulders once again felt as though they were touching my ears. My skin was breaking out from the "toxicity" of the situation. I felt uneasy and had trouble sleeping once again. I felt anxiety. I felt the lack of air.

I began to read self-help books, meditate, write in my journal and reflect once again to make the right choice for me. As soon as I made that decision I noticed I no longer had the stiff neck, my skin improved and I was back to running long distances again.

The teacher also showed me that I am filled with poetry that helped me release my emotions. It was so cathartic to write the words on paper. Even though tears would fall down my cheek as I penned them into my journal, they were a form of release. I take joy in knowing they now live on in this book to help others in times of sadness.

So my updated epilogue is to state - we are human. I could have just deleted the prior text in the Epilogue and pretended it never happened.

However, my friends, that is not life. The road bumps I am currently hitting are a necessary part of my journey. They will serve my soul and encourage further growth. I have once again "recalibrated" my idea of a destination on this journey. At first I cursed this teacher and begged for "no more lessons." Now I thank my teacher and gently remind myself the importance of patience.

Enjoy the journey,

Lorraine :)

ABOUT THE AUTHOR

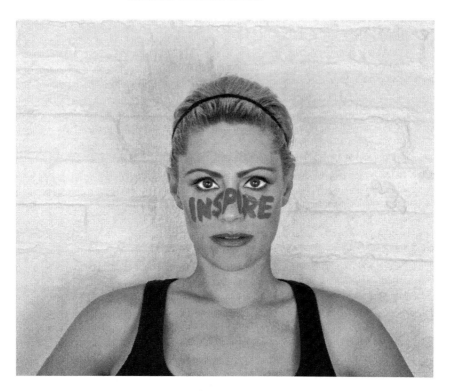

Lorraine Toth is a photographer, artist and now – author. She looks to always inspire others and bring out their inner beauty. She lives in her home in Upstate NY with her son, Johnny. Her daughter just graduated from Clarkson University and started her first full time job in Utica, NY.

To contact Lorraine's office, subscribe to her YouTube channel, find her on social media, meet her at events, book her for book signings and more, visit:
www.chooseahappyday.com

Please use hashtag **#run_book** when posting on social media so I can see you and say hi!

May your life be filled with air to help you cross all of the finish lines in life!

Have a happy day,
Lorraine

74214579R00089

Made in the USA
Columbia, SC
27 July 2017